LAMP
AND
LIGHT

LifeWay Press® / Nashville, Tennessee

ISBN 978-1-4627-6181-4
Item 005795934

Dewey Decimal Classification Number: 242.2
Subject Heading: DEVOTIONAL LITERATURE /
BIBLE STUDY AND TEACHING / GOD

Printed in the United States of America

Student Ministry Publishing
LifeWay Resources
One LifeWay Plaza
Nashville, Tennessee 37234-0144

We believe that the Bible has God for its author; salvation for its end; and
truth, without any mixture of error, for its matter and that all Scripture is
totally true and trustworthy. To review LifeWay's doctrinal guideline, please
visit www.lifeway.com/doctrinalguideline.

WHAT'S THIS?

What you hold in your hands has the potential to change your life. Not because of any clever devotional thought or activity, but simply because the Word of God is the focal point of every page. For a Christian, the Bible is the lens through which we should see all of life. Its pages are full of life-giving encouragement and instruction. Psalm 119:105 says, "Your word is a lamp for my feet and a light on my path." This truth is what makes every moment you spend in God's Word so important.

This devotional book is formatted to help you dive into God's Word for thirty days. We encourage you to take this book with you wherever you go—it can fit in your back pocket or inside your backpack. While the daily reading only takes a few minutes, you can ponder the questions long after you close the book. Highlight, draw, or make notes all through this book as you discover more about the character of God and His calling on your life.

Finally, memorize His Word. Say each day's verses over and over until you have a handle on the truth presented in each one. Once you feel confident you know those verses, try writing them out from memory.

We believe you were created to glorify God with your everyday life. Our hope is that diving into His Word will become an integral part of your daily routine. The Lord will use your time with Him to shape your character and guide your decisions.

DAY 01

Your word is a lamp for my feet and a light on my path.

PSALM 119:105

Like many kids in the southeastern United States, I grew up hunting and fishing with my dad. I love being outdoors. There's something about standing in the middle of the woods that inspires me. But also like many other kids, I was afraid of the dark—and nothing scared me more than being alone in the woods in the dark.

When I first started hunting by myself, Dad would drop me off and I would sit in a blind. And sit. And sit. All alone. Then Dad would return to pick me up when it was time to leave. Thankfully, he always gave me a flashlight. Hunting into the evening meant walking back to the truck in the dark, and the flashlight gave me courage. It clearly lit my path so I wouldn't stumble. I could shine it in the direction of any spooky sound and see what was there. It always helped me reach my destination safely. That's exactly what God's Word does for us.

Read Psalm 119:105. The psalmist describes what God's Word is like: a lamp and a light. God's Word lights our path, showing us which way we should go. His Word gives us courage to know that even though we may feel like we are walking in the dark, we have the promises of God to rest on and His Word to light our way (Joshua 1:9.) When we are afraid, we can turn to the Bible for comfort and reassurance that He is who He says He is (Psalm 23). When we feel alone, His Word tells us He never leaves His children (Psalm 139:7-12).

The flashlight I used while hunting provided me with enough light to reach the safety of our truck. In the same way, God's Word provides us with all the "illumination" we need to live in a godly manner, lighting our way so we can see His path and the best way to walk it.

01 **What fears do you have (besides the dark)?**

02 **Who or what do you seek comfort from when you are afraid? How does that help you face your fear?**

03 **How can you make God's Word a lamp and light to your path when you feel like you are in the "dark"?**

04 **What's one way you would like God to light your path this week? Ask God to shine His light on that one thing.**

But as for you, continue in what you have learned and firmly believed. You know those who taught you, and you know that from infancy you have known the sacred Scriptures, which are able to give you wisdom for salvation† through faith in Christ Jesus. **2 TIMOTHY 3:14-15**

Every generation has their flash-in-the-pan fads—clothes (parachute pants—ask your parents), stunts (planking), or games (bottle flipping)—that go the way of pogs. Wait, you don't know about pogs? Pogs literally dominated the mid-Nineties. Players would stack pogs, cardboard discs with an image on one side, hit the stack with a "slammer," and keep any discs flipped picture side up. Everybody played with pogs until, practically overnight, nobody did ... and a multi-billion dollar industry vanished.

Can you believe the Bible went the way of pogs at one point? In 2 Kings 22, the High Priest Hilkiah ran across this musty old Book of the Law while cleaning the Temple. He and King Josiah read it and realized they were all in mega trouble since they were doing, like, absolutely nothing God commanded.

Read 2 Timothy 3:12-17. Humans are a lot like Dug, the lovably flawed dog from the movie *Up* who would drop everything the second he glimpsed a squirrel. In hard times, we don't just take our eye off the ball, we tend to run off the field and pretend the game never existed.

That's why verse 14 says to "continue in what you have learned and firmly believed." Distractions entice us away from following God. The truth is that we could eventually forget God just like the people of Josiah's day unless we continue to study the Bible, spend time in prayer, and remain in Christian community. Don't risk treating the Son of God like a fad—especially since He is guaranteed to came back.

MY RESPONSE

01 **When do you find it easiest to "forget" God and His Word?**

02 **What does this struggle say about the current state of your relationship with God?**

03 **According to 2 Timothy 3:12-17, what benefits come from remaining in God's Word?**

04 **Which of those benefits is most important to you and how would its presence in your life improve your relationship with God?**

DAY 03

"... so my word that comes from my mouth will not return to me empty, but it will accomplish what I please and will prosper in what I send it to do." ISAIAH 55:11

How's your memory? Memorizing scientifficult words for your biology test or lines for a play can take weeks of daily practice. Typically, we memorize the things we enjoy returning to repeatedly, like that favorite movie you've seen a dozen times or that sick tune ruling the top of your "most played" list. Or maybe it's a passage from your favorite dog-eared novel, like "I do not like green eggs and ham, I do not like them Sam-I-Am." (Ha! Gotta love Dr. Seuss.)

No matter what you've memorized, it falls woefully short of memorizing the Bible since God's Word literally transforms lives. I'm not talking about just giving someone a new perspective or inspiring them to accomplish something. The Bible turns a person from a murderer to an evangelist (Paul), a fisherman to a theologian (Peter), a prisoner to a ruler (Joseph), or a literal corpse into a living, breathing person (Lazarus). Sure, pop culture can transport us to different worlds or enrich our lives in surprising ways, but it will never come close to the culture-shaping, life-giving, Holy Spirit-inspired impact of God's Word.

Read Isaiah 55:6-11. That's why the Bible is the only thing truly vital to memorize. There's nothing wrong with having a song stuck in your head or a movie quote jumping to your lips. But if you're not committing Scripture to memory, you're missing out on weaving the very wisdom of God into the fabric of your life. God's Word is the only writing that never returns empty and always accomplishes what God desires. It's the very wisdom of God whose ways and thoughts are far beyond our own.

MY RESPONSE

01 **How might memorizing Scripture prepare you for difficult situations you encounter in life?**

02 **What's your biggest hurdle to memorizing Bible verses?**

03 **What methods do you use to memorize things for school? How might these methods help you remember more of God's Word?**

04 **What is one verse of Scripture you will commit to memorizing this week? Start by writing it here:**

DAY 04

> *... but in your hearts regard Christ the Lord as holy, ready at any time to give a defense to anyone who asks you for a reason for the hope that is in you.* **1 PETER 3:15**

Back before the Internet (ask your parents), it took a long time for word to get out about things. There was little concern about movie spoilers beyond a loud-mouthed friend or about an embarrassing photo spreading beyond your family reunion.

Today, news blazes through social media like wildfire. Be it a disaster in a foreign country, shocking twist on a hot TV show, or goofy misstep your friend just happened to video, it seems like everyone is compelled to talk, share, and dissect every tidbit great and small.

That's how it should be about Jesus. If you trust Him with your salvation, read His Word, and see your relationship with Him transform your life, you should jump at the chance to talk about Him. In fact, people should simply see the change Jesus has made in you.

When they ask what's different, you should be ready. That doesn't mean you need to have an answer for every possible theological question. You must be prepared to be open and honest. Even though Jesus' impact on your life will be tremendous, you will be tempted to deflect, even pretend like nothing's changed. (That's what Peter did before the rooster crowed.) You must resist this urge and boldly give a "reason for the hope that is in you."

You cannot keep what God reveals to you in His Word secret—especially the good news about His Son, Jesus. Be ready like Philip was in Acts 8 when he met a high-powered Ethiopian government official. Philip was unashamed and excited to share, and the life of the official (as well as the nation of Ethiopia) was changed forever.

01 Why does God bother using us to share the good news about Jesus?

02 What do you find most difficult about being "ready at any time" to tell someone about Jesus?

03 Who are you most frightened to share the Word of God with? How would knowing Jesus improve that person's life?

04 How could regularly praying for that person as well as your "preparation" help you both?

DAY 05

The entirety of your word is truth, each of your righteous judgments endures forever. PSALM 119:160

The United States Constitution is revered as one of the crowning achievements in human thought. It serves as the foundation for our laws and governmental structure and has been admired and emulated around the world as a template for democracy. Despite all this, the Constitution still got it horribly, horribly wrong in Article 1, Section 2, Paragraph 3, where it valued slaves as only three-fifths of a person.

That's right. Until reversed by the Thirteenth and Fourteenth Amendments, the document that rose from the Declaration of all men created equal, that shrugged off tyranny and established democracy throughout the land, deemed some people as less than human. Even man's greatest writings get things wrong. They eventually disappear from the face of the earth (unless your name is Shakespeare) or get altered (the Constitution).

Read Psalm 119:153-160. People ignore, dismiss, and ridicule God's Word, but it is the only book in history that continues to be proven correct by archeology, science, public policy, and individual lives. Those who live by God's commands find life abundant today and for eternity. Those who don't will one day be proven not only wrong, but in deeper trouble than our mortal minds can attempt to imagine.

Take a moment to praise God by drawing close to Him and His Word.

MY RESPONSE

01 How have you personally (or people you know) experienced criticism or difficulty for believing in and following **God's Word?**

02 What is the most compelling argument against God's Word being true and how do you address that?

03 What can you do to strengthen your trust in God's Word?

04 How can you respectfully respond to someone who disagrees with God's Word while remaining **faithful to its truth?**

DAY 06

God—his way is perfect; the word of the Lᴏʀᴅ is pure. He is a shield to all who take refuge in him. **2 SAMUEL 22:31**

"Refuge." It's a word we rarely say but constantly do. What? Don't think you've taken refuge lately? You take refuge in something when you rely on it for protection. Cold? You take refuge in your North Face jacket. Tornado? Bet I find you taking refuge in a basement. Daily life? Hopefully your refuge is in God's Word.

That one might sound churchy, but we all take refuge when life gets tough. Unfortunately, when storms hit, the vast majority seek refuge in social media, drugs, consumerism, romance, etc. These fleeting ports of refuge don't actually protect us, though. They may numb us for a time, but ultimately leave us open to getting hurt even worse.

Read 2 Samuel 22:29-31. What's the first description that pops into your head when you think of David from the Bible? Probably "king" or "shepherd." Maybe "poet" or "slingshot enthusiast." The word that applies when reading these verses is "warrior." David went into life-threatening battle time and again. He engaged in battle from childhood (facing lions and literal giants) until his death. Yet after surviving another of his many military campaigns, David didn't boast. Instead, he sang a song about God as his perfect refuge.

David knew his strength and protection came from God. Everything God said in His Word, every promise and command, was trustworthy enough for David to follow into battle under threat of death.

You may not feel like a warrior, but I bet you feel like you're entering into battle some days. We're part of a spiritual war raging all around us whether we know it or not, which is why it's important to trust in God's Word, the only true source of refuge on the planet.

01 **Why doesn't God just shield us from everything that's bad in life?**

02 **Where do you typically take refuge when you get stressed, scared, or hurt? What effect does that refuge have on you?**

03 **What prevents you from turning to God's Word during tough times?**

04 **How could you seek refuge in God's Word in times of stress, fear, or pain? What lasting impact might that have on your life?**

I have not departed from the commands from his lips; I have treasured the words from his mouth more than my daily food.
JOB 23:12

Ever had a "conditional" friend? They're around when times are good, a blast to have at parties or for a late night Taco Bell run. But they seem to disappear when there's work to be done. You don't even consider asking them deep questions or for advice. And forget about when actual trouble hits—they're gone before you can say, "Help."

I can't help but wonder if God ever feels that way about us. We're ready and waiting by His side when He's passing out blessings. While the good times roll, we're tight with God—His dedicated wingman. At least until a storm blows in. Then it's sayonara, God—until He starts doling out the spiritual swag. Then we're all chummy again.

While I assume you've lived that way at times, I know I have. But when I add up all my worst days, they still can't touch what Job endured. He lost his entire family and possessions in one day before losing his health in another. Despite his overwhelming physical, emotional, and spiritual turmoil, Job not only remained true to God's Word, he continued to treasure it.

Read Job 23:10-14. No matter what life throws at you, God is in control. His love and plan for us is not conditional. When the world around you goes absolutely bonkers, you can be sure His will shall be done. That's why God's Word is a treasure more valuable than our possessions, relationships, and physical health.

I don't wish any Job-like occurrences in you life. I do, however, pray you reach for Job-like devotion to God and His Word. It will serve you perfectly now and for eternity, no matter what comes your way.

01 **When hard times hit, do you draw close to God or question His love for you? Explain.**

02 **What truths about God and Job do you see in Job 23:10-14?**

03 **Which of these truths do you need to incorporate into your life? How will you do that?**

04 **Think of the friends in your life. How does a friend who's there for you no matter what reflect God's love?**

Let the word of Christ dwell richly among you, in all wisdom teaching and admonishing one another through psalms, hymns, and spiritual songs, singing to God with gratitude in your hearts. **COLOSSIANS 3:16**

"Dwell" is an interesting word. It's different from simply visiting a place, like going on vacation to see all the famous tourist attractions and cities or camping in a beautiful spot. It's even different from places you hang out a lot, like your friend's room or your favorite coffee shop. You don't even "dwell" at you grandparents' house, no matter how long you visit.

The place you "dwell" is where you live, sleep, keep all your belongings, and (hopefully) feel safe. It's where you can be yourself, completely comfortable and honest with the people you love and who love you most. There is something intimate and special about where you dwell.

Read Colossians 3:16-17. It's no accident we see "dwell" used here. We aren't supposed to merely visit God's Word, acknowledging it for its beauty, superiority, or unique qualities before moving on to the next tourist trap. We are called to dwell with the Messiah and His Word, feeling as comfortable and at home in them as we would in our own beds.

This doesn't happen immediately. Just like it takes time to feel completely comfortable after moving into a new house, we must spend time with Jesus and His Word, growing accustomed to both. The difference in dwelling with them—you can never find the end. While you can explore and understand every nook and cranny of your home, you will never run out of rooms to explore in Jesus' character or His Word. And you will never find a safer place to dwell.

MY RESPONSE

01 **What's your favorite place to "dwell"? Why?**

02 **How is dwelling in Christ and His Word similar to dwelling in a home? How is it different?**

03 **How might dwelling in Jesus and His Word change someone's perspective in both good times and bad?**

04 **What small change could you make in your schedule to create time to dwell in God's Word daily?**

DAY 09

This book of instruction must not depart from your mouth; you are to meditate on it day and night so that you may carefully observe everything written in it. For then you will prosper and succeed in whatever you do. JOSHUA 1:8

"Stick with the game plan!" I can't tell you how many times coaches shout this to their players. When we watch a sport, we only see a tip of the iceberg that's formed by hundreds, even thousands of hours spent in practices, scrimmages, meetings, and studying film.

All of this time and energy is poured into crafting and executing the perfect game plan for victory. As you can imagine, when a player veers from the plan, coaches can get pretty upset. (It can be funny watching a coach flip out on the sideline—unless they're yelling at you.)

Read Joshua 1:8. One reason God gave us His Word is for instruction, almost like a game plan. When we step back and look at the big picture of human history and where we stand in it, we look pretty small. That's why we have His Word, so we'll be knowledgeable and ready to execute His game plan, because each of us has a part.

But that requires some preparation on our part. Some study. Just like going over a game plan in sports, we must know God's Word in the same way. The x's and o's of this verse show that God's Word must...
- not depart from your mouth. That means being ready to tell others the "game plan" to help them move forward.
- be recited day and night. Memorizing the plan helps you know what to do and when.
- be followed. We will succeed when we follow God's plan for us and not our own.

Stick with God's game plan for your life. It's the sure path to victory!

MY RESPONSE

01 **Why do you think we have a tendency to trust our own plans over God's plan?**

02 **When has one of your plans failed? When has following God's plan brought you success?**

03 **How can you tell whether you are following God's plan or your own?**

04 **What kinds of things could you do to help yourself stick more closely to God's "game plan"?**

DAY 10

Sanctify them by the truth; your word is truth. JOHN 17:17

Everyone has a little "geek streak" in them, because everybody really loves something that could be considered embarrassing. You might absolutely love minecraft, Doctor Who, or plush dolls. My "geek" love is Star Wars. I love the movies, books, and used to collect the action figures. One of my favorite characters is the one and only Darth Vader. (His scene in *Rogue One* was awesome!)

One of the most iconic scenes in all of the Star Wars movies involves Vader and Luke Skywalker. It's not the intense lightsaber battle or the crazy force-propelled moves. It's the four simple words Vader spoke to Luke in *The Empire Strikes Back*: "I am your father." Luke is obviously stunned, hurt, and confused because up until this point he didn't know that Vader was his father; he only knew him as the villain. Now, he knows the truth, and it hurts.

Read John 17:17. Sanctification is the process of God teaching us to become more like Him. Many times that involves showing us blind spots or sin in our lives. Sometimes, the truth really hurts. Whenever God shows me truth that hurts, I think about Luke Skywalker. This was a really hard moment in his life. But if you are familiar with the movies, the painful truth of his situation ultimately helped him grow.

Thankfully, our heavenly Father is good and gave us His perfect Word. Know that when you turn to God's Word to find answers, He will give them to you. (See Matthew 7:7-8.) That said, be prepared for the truthful answers. They are not meant to harm or hurt you, but to help you and improve your life. Memorize John 17:17 and reference it often. Yoda would probably say "Good it is, filled with truth it will be, always."

MY RESPONSE

01 When was the last time learning the truth about something was difficult for you? How did you react?

02 How did knowing the truth ultimately help you grow?

03 In what ways has spending time in God's Word over the last couple of weeks helped you become more like Him?

04 What are some other things you can do to help you grow in your faith?

I have treasured your word in my heart so that I may not sin against you. PSALM 119:11

I love Dallas Cowboys Football. I wish I could say that I used to be obsessed when I was a kid, but the truth is I'm drinking coffee out of a Dallas mug right now, wearing a Cowboy Nation T-shirt, and looking at my Dak Prescott bobble head as I write this.

While my obsession hasn't changed, some of my habits have. I used to collect posters, signed footballs, and trading cards. I insisted my mom record every game on our VCR. I spent countless hours obsessed with America's Team. While I still love the Silver and Blue, I am much more careful with how much time I spend thinking, reading, and talking about them. Basically, I limit how much I treasure them.

Read Psalm 119:9-12. Everyone treasures something. This passage shows how important it is to make God's Word that treasure. Matthew 6:21 says, "For where your treasure is, there your heart will be also." If you consider the things you spend the most time doing, thinking about, or talking about, then that is what you treasure. Hopefully, God's Word is in that "most treasured" conversation. The Bible helps us obey God's commandments, keeps us from falling into sin, and teaches us about our heavenly Father.

Psalm 119:9 speaks to the temptation to look for happiness in the wrong things. Over time, false treasures slowly build up until our hearts are crammed full of worthless junk that will one day disappear.

Thankfully, you can replace your (ultimately trivial) treasures with the eternal treasure of God's Word, which is "living and effective and sharper than any double-edged sword" (Hebrews 4:12). Fill your heart with the only treasure that never loses value.

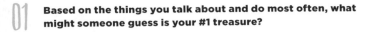

01 **Based on the things you talk about and do most often, what might someone guess is your #1 treasure?**

02 **How can that treasure be used to glorify God? (And if it can't, why are you holding on to it?)**

03 **What are some ways you can actively treasure God's Word more?**

04 **What positive impacts might treasuring God's Word have on your daily life?**

... because you have been born again—not of perishable seed but of imperishable—through the living and enduring word of God. For all flesh is like grass, and all its glory like a flower of the grass. The grass withers, and the flower falls, but the word of the Lord endures forever. And this word is the gospel that was proclaimed to you. **1 PETER 1:23-25**

Have you ever lied about something you loved to impress someone? (I know, you're perfect. Cough.) I had a huge crush on a boy in 7th grade. He played basketball, had blonde swooped hair and freakishly straight teeth without braces. He was a total middle school dreamboat. He grew up in the deep South and loved everything Southern, so I decided to love country music like he did. I googled country artists and tried hard to become a fan, but just couldn't bring myself to enjoy the music. I pretended it was my favorite, but my "love" for country music was nothing but a lie intended to get a boy's attention.

Read 1 Peter 1:22-25. Peter writes that because we are born again through the love of Jesus, we should extend that same love to others. But this isn't fake, romantic comedy love. Authentic Christian love is sincere, earnest, and flows from a pure heart. We are incapable of this type of love outside of abiding in Christ and dwelling in His Word. First John 4:19 says, "We love because he first loved us." His great love enables us to love others in this way, and it gives us the courage to continue loving even when we fail or others fail us.

My "love" for country music was made up entirely of empty words. The love that is found in Christ and throughout God's Word, and the kind of love Jesus calls us to extend to one another, is never fake. It is beautiful and pure and requires diligence to faithfully shower upon others. Thankfully, God's Word paints a vivid picture of Christ's love and helps us follow a path toward loving one another the way He loves us.

MY RESPONSE

01 When have you lied about something to impress others? What was the outcome?

02 How do you know the difference between fake and sincere love in your own heart?

03 How have you demonstrated Christ's sincere love for others?

04 How can God's Word help us love others? How could demonstrating His love more often change the world around you?

DAY 13

> **"Blessed be the LORD! He has given rest to his people Israel according to all he has said. Not one of all the good promises he made through his servant Moses has failed."** 1 KINGS 8:56

When I was growing up, my mom kept memorable items for each of her children in plastic boxes marked with our names. These included baby mementos, photos, school crafts, etc. Strangely, I continued this trend even after I moved out—probably to excess. Still, I love these boxes and now have seven filled with items that reflect different phases of my life.

The idea of being able to hold tangible evidence of the past in my hands and recall the memories associated with each item brings me a great deal of joy. I love that feeling of nostalgia. It isn't just about recalling the past, though. Remembering the past also helps me pay attention to the present and look forward to the future.

Read 1 Kings 8:56. The promised temple had finally been completed, and the people of Israel were ready to celebrate. Solomon fell to his knees and prayed before the Lord, recognizing His power and faithfulness. Then Solomon began to bless the people, immediately recalling the ways God had provided for them and how "not one of all the good promises He made ... failed." It was as if Solomon was going through his own "special box" of God's faithfulness to Israel.

My "special box" is now full of journals—pages filled with prayers of discouragement, joy, and a whole lot of impatience. Sometimes I like to slide this box out from under my bed and recall the ways God has kept the promises He has made to me in His Word. It always renews my hope to know and remember that God is who He says He is and that He will always keep His promises.

MY RESPONSE

01 **What promises has God kept for you?**

02 **What promises in God's Word are you still waiting for Him to keep?**

03 **What "nostalgic" reminders of God's promises, both those answered and the ones you still wait for, could you create?**

04 **How can recalling God's faithfulness to you in the past help you grow closer to God and trust Him more with your future?**

DAY 14

> *He answered, "It is written: Man must not live on bread alone but on every word that comes from the mouth of God."*
> **MATTHEW 4:4**

Have you ever been "hangry"? It's natural for your stomach to growl when you skip a meal, but go all day without eating? You can't think of anything but lasagna or waffle fries. You become lethargic, unreasonable, and weak. Eventually, you start to snap at the tiniest inconvenience.

Read Matthew 4:4. Jesus had been led by the Holy Spirit into the wilderness, and He hadn't eaten in 40 days. Can you imagine going 40 days without eating?! Talk about being hangry. I can picture Jesus' hands becoming shaky and His vision starting to blur. Maybe he even imagined the clouds were fluffy mashed potatoes.

Then Satan came in guns blazing, using Jesus' hunger to his advantage by asking Jesus to turn stones into bread. Even though Jesus had the power to make that happen, He responded by quoting Deuteronomy 8:3: "Man does not live on bread alone but on every word that comes from the mouth of the LORD." The Word of God was a pillar of strength for Jesus in the midst of temptation. Scripture provided a response to Satan's attack and a reminder of what Jesus knew to be true.

Satan knows our weaknesses, and he loves to use them against us. But we can emulate Jesus by using God's Word as a tool to fight temptation. This is why it's so important to memorize Scripture—to have God's truth ready in our time of need. His Word not only equips us when hard times come, but gives life, builds our faith, and makes us more like Christ. Whether you write verses on sticky notes, keep a journal, or set reminders on your phone, memorizing God's Word will help you recall His truth even in your weakest (or hangriest) moments.

MY RESPONSE

01 **Since Jesus was fully human, what are some other ways He might have been tempted during His lifetime?**

02 **What are your greatest temptations?**

03 **How do you currently respond when faced with temptation?**

04 **What are some practical ways for you to start memorizing Scripture today? How might that help you face temptation in the future?**

> **"The grass withers, the flowers fade, but the word of our God remains forever."** ISAIAH 40:8

Fresh flowers are some of my favorite things on earth. I love how they smell, how they are simultaneously wild and beautiful, and that they have the ability to brighten everything from a room to someone's day. They have always made me happy. As a little girl, I even used to get in trouble for messing up the neighbor's flower bed arrangements because I couldn't resist picking them. (Sorry!)

Though freshly-picked flowers are indeed very lovely, their beauty fades quickly. I am often guilty of keeping them far too long— sometimes until they start to smell weird. I'm always disappointed to throw them in the garbage and sad they couldn't make me happier a little longer. But flowers simply don't last. Even when planted in the ground, they will wither and die at the end of the season.

Read Isaiah 40:8. Thankfully, God's Word doesn't fade or wither away like a beautiful tulip or rose. Isaiah points out that although things of this earth can be good, they are never permanent. Only God's Word "remains forever." The Word of God doesn't need perfect weather conditions to grow or special water to stay alive in a vase to bring joy to others. His Word is eternal.

We often count on temporary things like flowers to bring us joy. But we find only fleeting pleasure in those things, beautiful as they might momentarily be. The Word of God is the only thing that doesn't shift or change. Even though it can affect our hearts in different ways as our circumstances change and we mature, the Bible remains constant. Rather than put your hope in a beautiful flower, physical appearance, or even a sterling reputation, look to God's eternal Word that will never fade or fail.

MY RESPONSE

01 What are some things in your life that only bring **temporary joy?**

02 Which of these "temporary" things do you need to place less **value on? How will you do that?**

03 How does knowing that God's Word is eternal and unchanging make a difference in the way you read the Bible?

04 How has God's Word changed your heart in the past? How would you like to see it impact your life **in the future?**

DAY 16

But be doers of the word and not hearers only, deceiving yourselves. JAMES 1:22

Learning how to play a musical instrument takes time. You have to take things slow, memorizing frets or chords before gradually moving to progressions and rhythms that eventually form songs. Not even prodigies can expect to pick up a guitar or a clarinet for the very first time and play it well. If learning an instrument is important to you, it takes discipline and must be a priority in your life.

I attempted to learn the piano by fiddling around on the keys and hoping they would magically come together to form a beautiful Coldplay song. But they never did because learning an instrument is about more than just knowing a melody. It's about making the commitment to learn a priority and practicing until your fingers hurt. In the same way, following Jesus is not just about knowing the truth, but about living out what God's Word says and making that the most important priority in your life.

Read James 1:22. This verse challenges us not to just read or listen to God's Word, but to take action and do what it says. So often, we know what needs to be done in order to know God and His Word—we just aren't willing to commit. It's not about obeying out of obligation. 1 John 5:3 says that His "commands are not a burden." God's children should naturally want to develop a deeper relationship with their heavenly Father. The more we read the Bible and let God's Word stir our hearts, the more we will know and understand Him.

There is a beauty in the way a song is formed. There is also tremendous beauty in the way the Word of God forms us, fine-tuning us to be more like God's glorious Son, Jesus.

01 **What is your biggest hurdle to practicing something that's difficult?**

02 **How do you typically fight through that hurdle? What are the benefits when you succeed?**

03 **What hurdles make it difficult for you to be a "doer of the word"?**

04 **What steps can you take this week to help you practice being a "doer of the word"? How will you make those steps a part of your daily life?**

> *Then Jesus said to the Jews who had believed him, "If you continue in my word, you really are my disciples. You will know the truth, and the truth will set you free."* JOHN 8:31-32

I love social media, but I get pretty tired of scrolling past all the blog posts that link back to a cousin's dog's dog walker's personal trainer's grandmother that I might have met at a Christmas service years ago. During a recent scroll marathon, I stumbled across an article about freedom. This time, the author actually presented some interesting ideas. She stated that humankind was created to experience freedom. The only thing was, her method for discovering and achieving that freedom felt off-kilter.

Read John 8:30-36. Jesus offered His followers a challenge. He pointed out that only those who meditate on His teachings can call themselves disciples. This was a charge to those weak in the faith to begin living out and abiding in His Word. Jesus then presented two promises. First, they would know truth. As God's children, He sees us as just that—children. Since we are still growing, God nurtures us through His promised truth, which is essential to our spiritual growth. The second promise was that truth leads to freedom, which releases us from bondage to sin and restores our relationship with God. Second Corinthians 3:17 tells us that anywhere the Spirit of God is present, there is freedom.

While the blogger suggested that freedom could be found within ourselves, leaning on our culture's mantra of "do what makes you feel good," true freedom only comes through Christ. Christ-centered freedom can actually break our enslavement to sin. And as we experience His promised truth, we will find freedom unmatched by anything the world offers.

MY RESPONSE

01 Do you feel truly free? What specific sin struggles do you need Jesus to release you from?

02 What does it mean to "continue in my word"? How can you do that more this week?

03 How might walking in Jesus' freedom help you recognize the empty promises of freedom our culture offers?

04 How can you proclaim the truth and freedom Jesus offers to those around you?

DAY 18

If you remain in me and my words remain in you, ask whatever you want and it will be done for you. JOHN 15:7

As a kid, it felt like asking my parents for things I wanted never worked. I don't mean food or water (they aren't savages!), but things like toys and candy. I even remember a time my dad wouldn't let me get a Baby Bottle Pop (remember those?) at the grocery store. I stuck it on the conveyor belt hoping he wouldn't notice. (Bad idea.)

We do the same thing with God all the time. We present Him with the stuff we want as something that will "help us with our Christian outreach" or "remind us of His goodness." Deep down, though, it's rooted in our own selfish desires.

Read John 15:1-8. Those who follow Christ and live out His Word will produce good fruit that can be used by the Father, while those who ignore His words will be separated from Him and thrown into the fire. (Yikes!) Then in verse 7 Jesus says, "If you remain in me and my words remain in you, ask whatever you want and it will be done for you."

Wait a second. I follow Jesus. That means I can receive as many Baby Bottle Pops as I want! Way to be an example of Christ, Dad!

Not exactly. As we continue abiding in Christ, producing fruit and becoming more like Him, our desires will become what He desires for us. The awesome part is, we won't be disappointed. All the worldly sweets our culture has to offer will seem like trash in comparison.

Jesus knows the temptation of earthly desires. He experienced them. He understands how hard it is to keep our minds focused on His will instead of our own. That's why you can ask Him without fear to change your heart so your desires will match His.

MY RESPONSE

01 What does abiding in Christ look like in someone's life? How are you currently doing that?

02 When have you noticed your selfish desires interfering with your relationship with God?

03 How might aligning your desires with God's simplify and bring more joy to your life?

04 What are some practical ways you can start abiding in Christ every day?

The Son is the radiance of God's glory and the exact expression of his nature, sustaining all things by his powerful word. After making purification for sins, he sat down at the right hand of the Majesty on high. HEBREWS 1:3

The sun is absolutely fascinating. It is a star one million times bigger than earth and has a gravitational pull so strong it keeps all eight planets (sorry Pluto) in place. It makes life on earth possible by giving us light as well as enabling plants to engage in photosynthesis, which ultimately sustains the food chain. Without the sun, earth would be a giant block of ice. Even in winter it provides the precise amount of heat the human race needs to stay alive.

Read Hebrews 1:1-4. The days of God directly revealing His truth through prophets had come to a close. God had now spoken through His Son, Jesus. Just like the sun sends radiant beams that sustain life on the earth's surface, God sent His Son to reach those in need of spiritual life. Jesus is "the exact expression" of God's nature. Without Him, we would have no way to survive eternally.

The thing about feeling the sun's warmth is that you must step outside to experience it. Sure, you can glance at your weather app, look out a window, or even have a friend tell you how it's the perfect day for a beach trip. But you can't truly experience how great the sun feels until you've stepped outside and felt the warmth on your skin.

Similarly, we must "step outside" and experience Jesus personally to truly understand His supreme goodness. If we sit inside and keep the doors of selfishness, doubt, and anger closed, we will never be affected by the life He brings. Jesus, the "radiance of God's glory," willingly shows us who He is. So go outside and experience Him!

MY RESPONSE

01 God could speak to us any way He wants. Why did He choose to send His Son?

02 How do God's Words sustain you?

03 In what ways does your life reflect the "radiance" of Jesus?

04 What are some ways you could help others "step outside" and personally experience Jesus' radiance?

Heaven and earth will pass away, but my words will never pass away. **MATTHEW 24:35**

You probably have some things you couldn't imagine living without. Take a minute to think about what that may include. Is it your always present iPhone that keeps you connected with everyone and everything? Maybe it's a certain sport, video game, or even your car.

Got a list in mind? Great. Now imagine all of those things have been suddenly wiped off the face of the planet. You reach in your pocket—no phone to be found. You run outside and find that your car has been replaced with a heaping pile of nothing. You're freaking out, right? How are you going to live without these essentials?

Read Matthew 24:32-36. Jesus was speaking about His future return, telling His followers to be prepared for the moment they will be taken from this world and into the next. He explained that none of their possessions would be taken with them. Because of that, Jesus challenged them to focus on what is important—His teachings and commands. These are the things that will last for eternity.

Since no one knows exactly when Christ will return, we should live every day with an eternal focus. By paying closer attention to the words of the One who reigns forever, we will naturally have less of a desire for the things around us that are temporary.

Are you keeping His Word in your heart? (See Psalm 119:11.) Are you meditating on it day and night? (See Joshua 1:8.) Jesus commands us to faithfully seek Him, so ask Him to help you put down that phone, stop polishing that car, or leveling up in that video game and look to His Word that will never break, fail, or disappear.

MY RESPONSE

01 **What makes it difficult for you to maintain an eternal focus?**

02 **How would an eternal focus improve your life?**

03 **How could your worldly "essentials" glorify God and build His kingdom? Which possessions can and need to be removed?**

04 **What steps can you start taking now to maintain an eternal focus in your daily life?**

DAY 21

"The one who believes in me, as the Scripture has said, will have streams of living water flow from deep within him." JOHN 7:38

Do you know exactly how drinking water contributes to your body's health? I did some research, and guess what? Water is amazing! Most of the water you take in leaves your body at some point, through sweat while you're getting jacked in the gym or tears while wrapped in your Snuggy watching "This Is Us." The majority passes through the kidneys, which filter just enough water into your bloodstream to join blood in its journey to the heart, making it possible for your body to move and release energy. That's how water keeps you alive.

Read John 7:37-39. Jesus was speaking to a crowd on the final day of the Festival of Tabernacles, a time for people to give thanks for that year's harvest. Each day of the festival, water was poured out at the altar to remind everyone how God miraculously provided water for Israel in the wilderness. Jesus, being the wise teacher that He is, used the topic already on everyone's minds to emphasize the necessity of believing in Him as the Messiah.

The "living water" Jesus spoke of in verse 38 is the Holy Spirit, who works in the lives of all believers. But that's not all. The Holy Spirit also leads us to reach out to others. At the time of this festival, most other religious groups had absolutely no desire to impact their surrounding community. Christianity was famous for extending life and blessings toward others, as it is today.

Just as water flows through the body to keep us moving, the Holy Spirit penetrates our souls to keep us moving toward Him and reaching out to others. When we follow Jesus, we are truly filled with life-giving water.

MY RESPONSE

01 **Your body constantly needs water. What are some ways you can constantly "rehydrate" your soul with spiritual water?**

02 **What happens when you don't regularly "rehydrate" through prayer and reading God's Word?**

03 **Water must seep into every square millimeter of your body. What areas of your life do you need to allow the Holy Spirit to seep into and lead you?**

04 **Who could you share this "living water" with? How will you do that?**

> *For the word of God is living and effective and sharper than any double-edged sword, penetrating as far as the separation of soul and spirit, joints and marrow. It is able to judge the thoughts and intentions of the heart.* **HEBREWS 4:12**

I was in Atlanta for a few days earlier this year attending a worship conference for college students. My group was a little late to the game when we booked our hotel, so instead of staying next to the event center, we ended up ten blocks away. Did I mention it was January?

We quickly figured out the fastest route to the event was walking—which meant facing a windchill of two degrees. Four layers of clothes beneath a large coat later, we made our ten-block trek. No matter how many layers I wore, every blast of arctic air cut straight to my bones.

Read Hebrews 4:12. Much like that frigid winter air slicing through my clothing, the Word of God cuts straight through all of our thoughts, notions, muck, and mess down to our heart and soul. Take, for instance, the woman at the well in John 4. It didn't take long for Jesus to cut straight to the heart of the matter, lovingly addressing the woman's sin issue of seeking fulfillment in people, not God, before leading her toward repentance.

Second Timothy 3:16-17 tells us that God's Word is useful for teaching, rebuke, correction, and training in righteousness. It cuts straight to the heart, not because the Lord is an angry Father yelling at His children, but because He is a good Father. (Good fathers don't let their kids play in the street while a Mack truck heads their way.) That sometimes means disciplining and encouraging or correcting and building up so that we become more like Jesus. God's Word may cut in the moment, but it heals and strengthens us for a healthy future with Him.

MY RESPONSE

01 When was the last time someone's words cut straight to your heart? Did they intend to hurt or help you? Explain.

02 What are some responses people have toward the Bible when it says something they don't want to hear?

03 When has reading the Bible "cut" you? How did you react?

04 How could you speed up the "healing" process in the future when God's Word cuts you, drawing attention to issues in your life you need to address?

DAY 23

"Don't think that I came to abolish the Law or the Prophets. I did not come to abolish but to fulfill. For truly I tell you, until heaven and earth pass away, not the smallest letter or one stroke of a letter will pass away from the law until all things are accomplished." MATTHEW 5:17-18

When I was a kid, Mom had a hard and fast rule at the dinner table: I had to clean my plate, which meant eating every scrap of food she gave me. One night I finished everything but the broccoli. (We've all been there, right?) As much as I tried to talk my way out of it, Mom wouldn't budge. Thirty minutes later I was gagging down cold broccoli and cheese. This led to a disgust for broccoli that lasted seven years, when I discovered cooked broccoli actually tasted good. In fact, it was one of my favorites! The reason I didn't like broccoli all those years before was because I kept letting it get cold. My perspective on broccoli dramatically changed.

Read Matthew 5:17-18. The first century Jews Jesus was speaking to were expecting the Christ—the Messiah—to liberate Israel from the tyrannical reign of the Roman Empire. But Jesus arrived on the scene and began preaching and teaching about the real reason He came: to fulfill the Law and the Prophets. No one has ever kept the law (Ps. 14:1-3), which means everyone is guilty (Jas. 2:10). Jesus came not to liberate us from our physical bondage to wicked rulers, but to free us from our spiritual bondage and give us life everlasting. Talk about a shift in perspective!

Our perspective on Jesus changes when we read God's Word. Without the Bible, we can create any mental image of Jesus we want. (That Jesus conveniently looks a lot like us, with our same goals and desires.) The true depiction of Christ is only found in His Word (John 1:1-18; Col. 1:15-20; Heb. 1:1-4).

MY RESPONSE

01 When has your perspective on something completely changed? What was the result?

02 Why is it so important to make sure we have the right perspective?

03 What factors can make getting the right perspective the first time difficult, especially when it comes to faith and the Bible?

04 How can you make sure you have the correct perspective concerning God's Word?

Then beginning with Moses and all the Prophets, he interpreted for them the things concerning himself in all the Scriptures.
LUKE 24:27

Taking tests can be stressful. With a high school diploma as well as a bachelor's degree, I've encountered my fair share of them. I would always get so frustrated when I missed questions that I knew I should have gotten right. Even though I knew that I should know the answer, I'd still end up guessing. I'd race back to my notes as soon as the test was over and realize I'd completely missed it. I had all the right information, but I still got it wrong when it came time to take the test.

Read Luke 24:13-35. On their walk to Emmaus, two of Jesus' followers were discussing everything that had happened over the past week—mainly Jesus' crucifixion and rumors of His resurrection. Along the way, they encountered a stranger and filled him in on all they had heard, revealing their concern that Jesus was not the Messiah as they had hoped. The stranger was shocked at their disbelief. He began interpreting all of the Law and the Prophets (aka our Old Testament), showing them where and how the Word clearly pointed to the things they were questioning. It had all been prophesied! All the information they needed was right there in plain sight, but they had missed it. (They nearly missed Jesus standing right in front of them, too!)

Just like these two followers, we are prone to miss the obvious. As Jesus explained, the entire Old Testament points to His virgin birth (Isa. 7:14), sinless life (Isa. 53:9), atoning death (John 3:14-17), and resurrection (Ps. 16:9-10). That's one of the reasons we must constantly return to God's Word. Human beings have a tendency to forget, but we can always look to His Word to remind us of who God is, what He has promised, and all He has done to save us.

MY RESPONSE

01 **When have you missed something obvious? How did you react when you learned your mistake?**

02 **Why is it easy to miss spiritual truths even when it's in front of you or written in God's Word?**

03 **What benefits come with returning to God's Word again and again?**

04 **How can the Holy Spirit help you become more observant and how might He give you opportunities to share those observations with others?**

DAY 25

In the beginning was the Word, and the Word was with God, and the Word was God. JOHN 1:1

Have you ever been out in public and heard the beginning of a song you recognized, but couldn't recall the name? As you hear the opening guitar solo, soft pad of piano, or pounding drum pattern, memories start to flood your mind. This song was your jam!

But you can't quite put your finger on what it's called.

Read John 1:1-5. What you see here is the "song intro" to John's Gospel, if you will. You feel like you've heard John's first few words before—but where? What or who is this "Word"?

This "Word" is Jesus, the Son of God and the second person of the Trinity. Jesus was not created; He has existed eternally because He is God.

"In the beginning..." also sounds familiar because you've read it in Genesis 1:1: "In the beginning God created the heavens and the earth." If you read carefully, you will also see a near mirror-image of creation. Jesus, the "Word," was there in the beginning as the agent of creation. The Father created everything through the Son, and all that was created was done so by Jesus alone. In Jesus, there is life and light. He entered the world to bring salvation to mankind and shine a bright light into darkness. Nothing will overcome Him or His kingdom.

The opening verses of John's Gospel remind us of a song we vaguely recognize. He's reminding us of who the "Word" is—Jesus, who was with God in the beginning of everything. Not because He was created, but because Jesus created everything. Jesus is the Son of God and He is God, and John wants to make sure that's a song we never forget.

MY RESPONSE

01 In what ways does John 1:1-5 mirror the creation account in **Genesis 1?**

02 Why is the fact that Jesus was with God in the beginning important? How does it affect your understanding of Him?

03 What other "song echoes" of Jesus do you hear around you in **everyday life?**

04 How might noticing Jesus' work in the world more often help draw you closer to Him as well as display Him more boldly to others?

DAY 26

For every one of God's promises is "Yes" in him. Therefore, through him we also say "Amen" to the glory of God.
2 CORINTHIANS 1:20

I was an annoying child. Having now witnessed many annoying children from an adult perspective, I've come to accept the fact that I am looking in a mirror. I was annoying for many reasons, but what got my mom the most was one constantly repeated question: "Really?"

"The lake is safe to jump in." "Really?"
"The lions in the zoo cannot eat you." "Really?"
"The Brussels sprouts taste good." "REALLY?"

Most of the time, Mom would simply respond with, "Yes, really," and that was enough. I just needed confirmation one more time that it was OK. I could trust her promises (except for Brussels sprouts).

Read 2 Corinthians 1:20. We have a heavenly Father who understands our need for assurance. Paul reminds us that every promise God ever made in the Bible was confirmed through Jesus. His perfect life and death on the cross is the fulfillment of all of God's promises, and it is in that truth that we find the promise of God's grace and mercy to us today. Jesus is the resounding "YES" to our question of "Really?"

"Yes, God really loves you."
"Yes, God really will forgive you."
"Yes, God really will provide for you."

There will always be moments when we question our circumstances: "Really?" But we can meet those moments with confidence that God will hold true to His Word. If He could send His Son to die for you, He will keep all His other promises, today and through eternity.

01 **Read 2 Corinthians 1 and focus on verses 15-22. What are the differences between the "Yes" of man and the "Yes" of God?**

02 **Think of a time when someone kept a promise they made to you. How did that affect your relationship with and trust in that person?**

03 **What biblical promises has Jesus already fulfilled?**

04 **How might trusting God to keep His promises change your attitudes and actions?**

DAY 27

God—his way is perfect; the word of the Lord is pure. He is a shield to all who take refuge in him. PSALM 18:30

Silver is purified by heating it to 1,450 degrees Fahrenheit. The entire process is much more complicated than simply setting it on fire. In my research, I came across words like "electrolysis," "cupellation," and "electroplated." I'm now satisfied with the knowledge that the metal workers who set silver on fire seem to be attempting to destroy it in every way possible.

But they aren't destroying it; they are purifying it. And after burning away every speck of dross (that's just a scientific word for "impurity," btw), they are left with nothing but pure, sparkling, precious silver.

Read Psalm 18:30. When the psalmist said that the Word of the Lord is "pure," he was actually using a term that refers to metallurgy, or the science of metals and their production. In the same way a metal worker puts silver through extreme heat to purify it, the Bible has been scrutinized and tested in every way possible. It is pure and without flaw. There is nothing in it that needs to be stripped away. Unlike the grime and debris that needs to be removed from silver, there is nothing to be removed from or added to the Bible that will make it more applicable to our lives or the world in which we live.

Because God's Word is true and perfectly pure, we can take refuge in Him and what the Bible says. It would be difficult to rest easy in a shelter that seems unstable or flawed. Thankfully, we can rest in assurance that the Word of our Lord has never fallen when attacked by those who would like to see it crumble, and it never will. No matter what fire people attempt to burn God's Word with, it will remain standing for eternity as a refuge for those who abide in Him.

01 **What reasons do people give for not believing God's Word is perfect and pure?**

02 **Which of these reasons is the hardest one for you to ignore? Who can you talk to so that you can learn to better respond to this reason in the future?**

03 **Why do you think people often feel compelled to add to or take away from the Bible?**

04 **What one way can you personally abide in God's Word and put its perfection to the test this week? How could that draw you closer to God?**

DAY 28

The revelation of your words brings light and gives understanding to the inexperienced. **PSALM 119:130**

I remember lying in my bed, screaming for my mom to come to my room. A nightmare had woken me up, and all I could see was darkness. I couldn't figure out where I was, and I was convinced that the monsters who had invaded my dreams were now surrounding me on all sides. I heard Mom turn the knob on my door, then the faintest crack allowed the hallway light to spill in.

That was when I realized I was, indeed, in my bedroom. The light chased away all the imagined monsters and ghosts, leaving me surrounded by my own comforting paintings and stuffed animals. All it took was the tiniest sliver of light to bring me clarity and comfort.

Read Psalm 119:130. God's Word opens the door and shines light into the darkness of our world. Looking through the filter of God's light always helps us better understand our circumstances. Sometimes God's light reveals something scary, like the enemies we face, but it will also show us how to prevail. There will be times when the world seems dark and confusing, but we have the Bible as a lamp for our feet (Psalm 119:105). His Word shows us how much He has done for us already, as well as His promises and plans for the future. It helps us realize just how much we need Him and how His love for us is unending.

One of the most beautiful things about the light of God's Word is how accessible it is to everyone. It doesn't matter how old or wise you are, we all have moments (or days or years) when we need guidance.

God's Word is a door to be opened. He will shine His light of knowledge, understanding, and clarity on any dark situation when you seek Him in His Word.

01 **When has God's Word been a light in a dark situation you were experiencing? Explain.**

02 **What might cause someone to remain in the dark, refusing to turn to the light of God's Word?**

03 **What dark situation do you need God's light to shine upon? How will you seek that light?**

04 **What dark situation is a friend or family member going through that you can shine God's wisdom upon? How will you do that this week?**

DAY 29

He said, "Rather, blessed are those who hear the word of God and keep it." LUKE 11:28

I had a friend who always bragged about being distantly related to Abraham Lincoln. It was her absolute favorite fact about herself. She would always pick biographies about Honest Abe for book reports, and she never failed to mention somewhere in the report that he was her great-great-uncle eight times removed. OK, I can't actually remember the exact relation. But I have no doubt about how proud she was to be one of Abraham Lincoln's descendants. It made me sad (and a bit jealous) that I wasn't related to anyone exciting.

Read Luke 11:27-28. The woman in the crowd was saying that Mary must be so blessed to be related to Jesus and to share that sort of closeness with Him. In the same way that I wished for a relationship like my friend's, this woman wished she could be like Mary and experience the blessing of being related to Jesus.

But Jesus says that those who listen to and abide by the Word of God are even more blessed than Mary! Through the Bible, we have an opportunity to know the very heart, mind, and character of God and attain a spiritual closeness with His only Son. By giving us His Word, God provided a way for all people, throughout all nations and for all time, to have a personal relationship with Him.

We should receive great joy from remaining in and living by the Word of God because it allows us to have a personal relationship with the Creator of the universe. In Luke 11:28, Jesus told the woman in the crowd (and us) to remember that the people who were physically related to Jesus were no more blessed than those who have a relationship with Him through His Word. We are, in fact, more blessed because of it!

MY RESPONSE

01 How has hearing and obeying God's Word blessed your life?

02 How can God's Word help someone form a relationship with Him? How are you taking advantage of that?

03 Can people who haven't heard or who don't follow God's Word be blessed? Explain.

04 What is one thing you can do this week to bless those around you?

How can a young man keep his way pure? By keeping Your word. **PSALM 119:9**

Have you ever been on vacation and seen those little guidebooks in hotel lobbies? They tell you about all of the area attractions, and they normally include a map to help you get where you want to go. My father loves these books. No matter how many times I try to convince him that using my smartphone would be a much simpler option, he absolutely cannot resist picking up a copy of the guidebook. He always says, "How am I supposed to know where I'm going if I don't have something that tells me how to get there?"

As much as my millennial mind tells me that the answer to his question is called an iPhone, part of me is forced to agree. How do I know how to reach my destination if there isn't anything that tells me how to get there? It often feels like life could use a guidebook—something that tells us how to wisely travel down each path. Luckily, we have that.

Read Psalm 119:9. We can use God's Word as a guide for how to live. If you desire a life that brings glory to God, a "way that is pure," then engage the Word of God. You don't have to question whether or not you can trust the Bible as a source of inspiration or knowledge. The Bible is God-inspired (see 2 Timothy 3:16) and worthy to be held as your standard for truth and goodness.

Unlike my father's beloved guidebooks, the Bible will never go out of date, become useless, or fail to speak into your life. Hebrews 4:12 says, "For the word of God is living and effective and sharper than any double-edged sword." As you grow in both physical age and spiritual maturity, God will continue to use His Word as a way to lead you and teach you how to live a pure life. And that's something not even an iPhone can do.

MY RESPONSE

01   **Where do you typically turn first when looking for guidance in life?**

02   **What keeps you from turning to the Bible for answers first (or at all) during your search?**

03   **What are some ways God could prove the value of His Word as a guide for your life?**

04   **How might putting His Word to the test improve your life and also draw you closer to God?**

WHAT'S NEXT?

CONGRATULATIONS on sticking with this and finishing 30 days of devotions! We believe the time you spent with God will have a lasting impact on your life.

Have you noticed any changes in what you think about or how you spend your time since starting this journey? Have you applied some of the truths you've discovered in the last 30 days? If so, how? What has been the result?

So, what's next? Do you have a plan for next month and the month after that? Here are a few suggestions to keep you grounded in God's Word:

- Read a chapter of Proverbs every day. There are 31 chapters so this plan will work no matter what month it is!
- Begin reading through one of the Gospels (Matthew, Mark, Luke, John) in the New Testament. Read a chapter a day or spend several days digging into each section. If you finish before the end of the month, start the next book.
- For more interactive devotions like the ones you found in this book, check out ec magazine at www.lifeway.com/ec.

Whatever you decide to do, make sure you are taking time every day to pray and read God's Word.

ACKNOWLEDGEMENTS

- Special thanks to the following writers: *Bryan Belknap, Hannah Letson, Josh Hunter, Brett Schultz, Anna Beth Shelton, and Hunter Gregg*
- Graphic Designer: *Amy Lyon*
- Team Leader: *Karen Daniel*
- Manager, LifeWay Student Ministry Publishing: *John Paul Basham*
- Director, Student Life: *Brad Barnett*
- Director, LifeWay Student Ministry: *Ben Trueblood*